The Power of You

Overcoming Narcissistic Manipulation

By

Beverly Latimer

Dedication

For My Daughters

Andrea and Aleicia.

Your love is the quiet strength behind every word. Your love fills every page. May you know your worth and chase your dreams with the courage and joy you inspire in me every day.
Love you to the moon and back.
Mom

Introduction

In today's contemporary world, narcissism has become both a psychological concept and a cultural narrative. This book looks at the multifaceted sides of narcissism. It involves more than vanity or self-absorption, encompassing a range of traits that impact relationships. Traits can be observed in various individuals, including leaders and influencers, that impact interactions and perceptions.

By drawing on psychological insights, this book investigates the factors that contribute to narcissistic behavior, the insecurities behind it, and how it can act both as a defense mechanism and as a manipulative tool. The objective is to provide readers with the knowledge to better understand and manage relationships involving narcissistic individuals.

Please take time to think about you what is being discussed, then write your answers and thoughts down. Use this book to refer, reflect and see how you have learned and grown.

Table of Contents

Being In A Relationship With A Narcissist

A key sign of narcissistic personality disorder is a deep lack of empathy. Usually, because of early childhood neglect, narcissists do not tend to reach the emotional developmental stage of truly being able to understand or sympathize with another person's experience. Instead, they remain stuck in their own personal world.

Such people are wrapped up in their own wants and needs, without the ability to put themselves in someone else's shoes or genuinely empathize. Generally, narcissists are harsh, unforgiving, and judgmental of others, and of course, incredibly selfish.

Instead of empathizing, understanding, or genuinely caring about others, narcissists prefer and even need the focus and attention to always be on them.

A narcissist needs to believe they are "special and different" and that they are always right. They can come across as arrogant and self-entitled. There is no denying that narcissists have this deep need—born out of insecurity—that drives them to act as if they are all-knowing, intelligent, or superior. Often, they may talk down to you or others in a condescending or belittling way.

Narcissists are incredibly egocentric and self-centered. To them, they are the center of the universe; therefore, their wants and needs are, as far as they're concerned, much more important than anyone else's. A narcissistic partner will usually pursue their wants and needs regardless of how it affects you or anyone else. They may also expect you and others to regard their interests and needs the same way they do. If you don't, they often become critical or judgmental. Narcissists are essentially very controlling, and you may find that your partner dismisses or belittles your own wants and needs, as if they do not matter.

You may already have evidence of this behavior or simply feel it in your gut. Either way, if your gut instinct is that you are being lied to or manipulated, it could be a strong sign that you are in a toxic relationship with a narcissist. Narcissists will go to great lengths to lie and manipulate in order to get what they want and to feed the admiration and attention that their fragile egos desperately crave. Over time, this can have a devastating impact on your emotional and mental health.

A relationship with a narcissist is full of ups and downs. It is often an "on and off" relationship fueled by constant drama.

Toxic relationships can feel addictive. They can feel both exciting and draining at the same time. Being in a relationship with a narcissist is a journey of endless ups and downs. The cycle of highs that feel intoxicating and lows that are painful and damaging. This pattern is a clear indicator of an unhealthy relationship. In fact, relationships with narcissists are characterized by instability and inconsistency, which can be draining to the core. Such relationships often result in increased stress, exhaustion, and burnout for the partner involved. In contrast, a healthy relationship feels safe and balanced, because frankly, it is.

Your partner will rarely, if ever, apologize or take responsibility for themselves or their actions. Narcissists very rarely do either of these things. Although at times, they may appear to apologize or accept responsibility, but it is almost never genuine. Usually, any apology or act of responsibility is just another form of manipulation that serves their own selfish needs and gains. In healthy relationships, both partners take responsibility for their actions, respect each other's boundaries, and apologize when necessary.

You may also notice that you feel more anxious in the relationship. Simply put, a healthy relationship should feel safe, fulfilling, nurturing, and supportive. However, if instead you feel trapped, oppressed, or constantly anxious, it is a sign of being in a toxic or unhealthy relationship—usually one involving a relationship with a narcissist. People with narcissistic tendencies purposely trigger fear and anxiety in you as a way of gaining power and maintaining control.

If you try to express how you feel or set a boundary, you may be told that you are being "too sensitive," "over the-top," demanding," "imagining things," "ungrateful," or even "crazy."

Narcissists do not respect other people's boundaries. What they want and need always takes priority. But you are entitled to your own personal boundaries. In healthy relationships, you feel safe and comfortable expressing them. Healthy relationships are built on clear and respected boundaries. These boundaries—your needs, preferences, and limits—are openly communicated, mutually understood, and honored by both partners.

When you are in a relationship with a narcissist, however, this is not the case. They prefer to be with someone who won't hold firm boundaries or stand strong in what is or isn't acceptable. Narcissists often push, test, and manipulate boundaries to always get their way.

You often feel like it's "my fault" and that nothing you do or say is ever "good enough."

Feeling "not good enough," along with anxiety, fear, guilt, or shame, is often synonymous with being involved with a narcissist. In many ways, nothing is—or ever will be—enough for a narcissist. They never have enough, and nobody or nothing is (or ever will be) enough as far as they're concerned. No external validation or achievement will ever heal or fill their deep inner emptiness. That is their issue and their responsibility—not yours.

What is your responsibility is working to understand this distinction, to build your own self-esteem, and to strengthen your sense of self-worth and boundaries. With healthy boundaries, you gain clarity about what is truly your responsibility and release the misplaced sense of blame or fault. In time, you can also let go of guilt and fully recognize that you are, in fact, good enough.

The relationship is adversely impacting your self-esteem and mental health. Toxic relationships with a narcissist can have a devastating and damaging effect on your self-esteem and mental health. Healthy relationships enhance your well-being, helping you feel safe and secure—not anxious, nervous, or as though you are walking on eggshells, which is usually the case in an abusive relationship.

You may feel as though you can't relax or be yourself when in a relationship with a narcissist. It's not uncommon to begin losing your sense of identity, as if you don't even know who you are anymore. In a bid to cope, many partners or relatives of narcissists turn to maladaptive coping strategies, such as alcohol or drug abuse, or develop controlling behaviors such as eating disorders or obsessive-compulsive tendencies.

Many people also end up seeking therapy for these issues or feeling concerned about their own mental health when, in reality, the root problem lies in the effects of a toxic relationship. When you step away from and end such a relationship, your self-esteem, positive mental health, and overall well-being can begin to be restored.

Narcissistic Personality Disorder (NPD)

NPD affects approximately 6% of the population. NPD involves grandiose thought patterns, an intense need for admiration, and an inability to empathize with others. While creating a healthy relationship can be challenging, in some instances it is possible. Individuals with NPD may struggle with respect due to their narcissistic tendencies. However, with the right tools and information, it is possible to learn how to live with a narcissist and build a healthier dynamic. Setting healthy boundaries and communicating effectively with this personality type are key to maintaining a mutually beneficial relationship.

It's important to understand that people with NPD display an exaggerated sense of self-importance and entitlement. These traits make it difficult for them to respect those around them. Interactions with a narcissistic person can become more manageable when you understand this limitation, as it helps you develop realistic expectations about how you might be treated. The root cause of their disrespectful behavior often stems from a constant craving for admiration and validation from others.

To avoid being manipulated by someone living with NPD, you must be confident and assertive. Knowing how to make a narcissist respect you means standing up for yourself while staying composed during disagreements and confrontations. Behaviors like this make you less likely to be targeted as someone who can be easily controlled or taken advantage of. Use reinforcing statements that are based on facts or observations, without attaching personal feelings.

Understanding how to establish boundaries with a narcissist is essential. Individuals who display narcissistic traits often ignore the feelings and needs of those around them. By clearly communicating your limits and consistently enforcing your boundaries, you can minimize confrontations. Additionally, recognizing when it is necessary to sever ties if the behavior becomes harmful or toxic is part of ensuring that a narcissist respects you.

Make your expectations crystal clear and known by:

- Communicating your boundaries calmly and firmly.
- Expressing consequences if your boundaries aren't respected.

- Being consistent about not allowing your boundaries to be crossed.

How Do I Work on Myself?

The first thing one needs to evaluate is what my relationship is with myself?

"Internal behaviors" refer to thoughts, feelings, and emotions that occur within a person and are not readily observable by others. "External behaviors" are actions or expressions that can be seen by others—essentially, the outward manifestation of a person's internal state. In simpler terms, internal behaviors are what someone is thinking or feeling inside, while external behaviors are what they physically do or say.

What affects me internally?

____

____

____

____

What affects me externally?

____

____

____

____

What is holding me back from achieving what I want?

____

____

____

____

Focus only on the victory.

What forces you to succeed?

____

____

____

____

Think about the positive outcome. See yourself as successful, and let go of negative thinking. Tap into the positive possibilities.

DO NOT SETTLE!

Settling for less means accepting something that is less than what you want or deserve. Settling can lead to feelings of disappointment, a lack of fulfillment, or feeling held back.

Consider why you might be accepting less:

- Fear of taking risks?
- Lack of fulfillment?
- Denial?

Settling for less means you have convinced yourself to stay with someone or something even though you know you can do better.

Ask yourself: are you afraid of taking risks?

Do you lack experience outside your current environment and company?

Do the benefits outweigh the negatives?

If you feel you deserve better, but this also feels right, then here you are! You can settle.

Sometimes you may have all the things in the world and still feel no satisfaction.

So, is it better to achieve satisfaction rather than simply have all the good things in life?

What Do You Want?

Forgive yourself for staying in an abusive, unhappy situation. Forgiving a narcissist involves acknowledging the manipulation that occurred.

Avoid directing anger at yourself for staying in the relationship, and refrain from projecting it onto others.

Identify the triggers that lead to unwanted behaviors.

Express your genuine desires and pursue them, provided they do not harm you or others.

Find Out Who You Really Are!

Imagine being at the beach. You approach the water's edge and place your feet in the ocean, feeling refreshed. You gradually walk into the water to cleanse yourself. You dive into the water through an approaching wave and emerge on the opposite side. Next, observe the conditions to identify an appropriate wave to ride. Once you emerge from the wave, consider whether your technique meets the intended outcome (focused, joyful, happy, etc.).

Think About This!!!

What is my purpose?

What's not working for me?

How To Know If You Are 'Settling For Less' In Your Relationship?

- Are you losing yourself trying to please the other person and grab their undivided attention?

____

____

____

____

Are they not fulfilling your needs, and are you compromising your values too often?

____

____

____

____

- Is it possible for you to be open to major, unexpected changes?

____

____

- Are you ready to let go of the steering wheel and allow things to unfold naturally?

____

____

____

____

- Do you remain calm and appreciative of life even when things go wrong?

____

____

____

____

Imagine you are experiencing a difficult period, and Johnny/Jane approaches you. He or she speaks comforting words and then says, *"I am the only person who really cares about you."*

That's a lie!

Do They Really Care About You?

• Do they devalue you?

• Do you feel nervous, anxious, or is your self-confidence shaken?

Are you aware that projection is a behavior often observed in narcissists? Projection occurs when they attribute their own thoughts, feelings, or characteristics to another person instead of acknowledging or addressing them within themselves. Projection is a defense mechanism and is compounded further when associated with trauma and denial. If you project something onto others, it means you see it somewhere in yourself. Most people are not prepared to admit it. Narcissists often use projection as a way to dump their issues onto others.

How Should You Respond?

- Stay calm.
- Recognize and acknowledge the projection.
- Notice and decide how you are feeling.
- Set boundaries.
- Disengage if you must.

Do the projections below happen in your relationship with your narcissist?

- They think you are fighting every time you express your feelings. (Yes/No)
- They ignore or belittle your emotions. (Yes/No)
- They purposely misunderstand or misinterpret you. (Yes/No)
- They make you feel bad about sharing your thoughts or feelings. (Yes/No)
- They confuse you or manipulate you with mind games. (Yes/No)

- They treat you like you are not important to them. (Yes/No)
- They don't show concern when you're feeling weak or sad. (Yes/No)
- The relationship lacks equilibrium, as you consistently contribute more than you receive in return. (Yes/No)
- They do not show love and keep themselves emotionally distant. (Yes/No)
- They make you feel worse rather than supporting or comforting you. (Yes/No)
- They smile in your face but talk negatively about you behind your back. (Yes/No)

Why Does It Seem Like Narcissists Get Away With Everything?

They only *seem* to get away with everything. If you are around one long enough, you'll see they don't. The problem is, they don't show their suffering like others.

When you confront their abusive behavior or hold them accountable for their actions, narcissists dislike being questioned. When they feel like they are losing control and authority over people or situations, they react strongly. They do not want to lose control or authority over anyone.

Individuals displaying narcissistic traits may become upset if others do not acknowledge or respond to their attempts at manipulation or gas lighting. When someone goes against them, they feel insulted. Narcissistic individuals may experience distress if their anger, needs, and desires are not acknowledged or addressed.

When you adhere to ethical principles and refuse to support actions that go against your values, narcissists become frustrated because they want your obedience. Criticism and truth have a corrosive effect on narcissists—they cannot handle them.

Individuals with narcissistic traits often experience anxiety about being exposed. They are motivated to maintain their reputation and public image at any cost. When their errors are pointed out, it challenges their constructed persona. Additionally, rejection or being ignored can result in feelings of insult and humiliation. A narcissist may hold resentment as a consequence, experiencing an overwhelming sense of hatred, contempt, and disdain for you—not because of any wrongdoing on your part, but because you dared to reclaim your own power. You dared to assert your rights, set boundaries, and demand the respect you deserve.

Most narcissists cannot keep lifelong friends. Most narcissistic families will create distance and buffers to keep them away.

Many have at least one narcissistic parent who would abuse them until the day they die. Narcissism is not a choice. It develops in the first years of life, when personality is formed. NPD is created because of severe and long-term neglect, hurt, and abusive upbringing.

The long-term neglect of a child is severe enough for the child to develop an alter ego. With this alter ego, the damage from neglect, indoctrination, enforcement, and other forms of abuse is diminished, since the narcissist works well at self-protection. This new self is emotionally underdeveloped. To be able to manipulate and take very good care of the alter ego, the ability to feel empathy is lost.

Feelings that protect the new self are enhanced in the narcissist. To manifest narcissism, deep in his or her personality, feelings of grandiosity, entitlement, and of being the best or the smartest (or the most beautiful) are greatly heightened.

This new façade is paper thin. If this façade is removed, it reveals a weak and scared person, filled with guilt and shame. The person behind the alter ego feels unworthy of a relationship based on real love, friendship, and respect.

Being a narcissist is not a choice. It is self-protection built in the unconscious mind of the narcissist. NPD has forced its way forward in order to protect against the horrible truth of the person's living conditions and imperfections. It is the child's rescue, because the child was not resilient enough to survive mentally without its alter ego—narcissism. The lack of sympathetic emotions ensures the narcissist's ability to focus on their own needs.

Most narcissists will get the upper hand in court at the beginning, but if you stick with it, stay true to yourself, never give up on your children, and show the narcissist no remorse, the narcissist will usually end up losing everything in the end.

Narcissists are incapable of long-term relationships and will never feel love or feel like someone truly loves them. But you can feel love.

Narcissists have a hole in them that no amount of supply will ever fill, and so they spend their entire life never feeling complete. The things narcissists care about are very self-serving and superficial, but they are a reflection of their deep insecurity and the emptiness they carry inside.

Image

The first thing that means the world to a narcissist is their image. The way they look, dress, and present themselves—image is everything to them. Sociopaths often don't care about their appearance or how others perceive them, so they might go to a shop looking disheveled and make an effort only when it suits them. But narcissists, especially in their prime years, are obsessed with looking good and appearing to have it all. The covert narcissist, specifically, is very strategic with what they allow people to see. When they walk out of the door, they see it as a performance. Everything must align with their desired image.

Narcissists invest time, money, and energy into looking good and making people think highly of them. Everything they do is meant to improve their reputation and status. The only people who truly see behind the disguise are those closest to them—partners and children.

Narcissistic Supply

The second most important thing to a narcissist is their narcissistic supply, often derived from the false image they project. They need attention, compliments, and praise to feel good about themselves. They need to know they are loved by the masses and held in high esteem. They also need dark narcissistic supply, which they get from hurting and betraying the people they claim to love. To gain this, they deceive people into entering relationships with them.

The effort narcissists put into obtaining their narcissistic supply shows how important it is to them. For narcissists, people are just a means to an end. This is why they cannot genuinely love or care for anyone; it is about power and control. Supply makes them feel strong.

Money and Power

The third thing a narcissist cares about is Money and Power. Money helps them boost their fake image and buy more and more things to distract themselves from their inner misery. They refuse to accept that money cannot buy happiness, so they chase success to gain more.

They have also realized that with more money, they can control more people. They use finances to keep certain people tied to them. And with money, as with everything else, they can never have enough and are never satisfied.

Narcissists enjoy controlling others and being feared, and money grants them even more power. They are weak, insecure, and highly dependent on others to make them feel better or distract them from their inner turmoil. This is why they cling to their fake image—it gives them access to more people. And more people mean more Narcissistic Supply as it is their fuel for life.

Finally, money and power are tools that help them gain greater control, maintain their image, and secure further Narcissistic Supply.

All you must do is get away from the narcissist and begin to heal. You will start to feel complete again. The anger you feel—wanting the narcissist to suffer as much as you have—is understandable, but it is not healthy for you. Let that go. Do not hold onto the suffering anymore.

Remember, the more you think about them and what they've done, the more they win.

Don't let them win anymore.

Did you notice that after you left a narcissist, he or she is now texting you? Do you know why?

A narcissist needs to maintain control over every situation, even when they're not physically present. To ensure you remain under their influence, one of the most effective tools they use is texting. When they can't control you directly, they manipulate you through their texting habits.

Narcissists have little respect for boundaries, especially when it comes to your time and personal space. They prioritize their need for endless attention and always demand it. Any attempt on your part to divert attention is seen as a betrayal. This leads to constant texting, often with intense interactions, making you feel increasingly anxious and dependent on their validation.

Despite being constantly on their phones, often engaging with others, they intentionally ignore you, making you feel invisible. They ignore your messages online, showing you that you're not a priority. This silent treatment eats away at your self-esteem, forcing you to question your value.

Sometimes, they engage in a warm conversation that makes you feel seen and connected. These moments are particularly common when you are close to the devaluation stage of the relationship. Whether it's because they are in a good mood or because they need something from you, their motive is usually manipulative.

Sending a short message like "Good morning" and then disappearing is a tactic to provoke an emotional response and create uncertainty in the relationship. This behavior exploits power dynamics, leaving you confused and waiting for their next move.

Narcissists panic and become scared when they lose control over you. For them, relationships are all about control. When they realize they cannot control you, they feel powerless and helpless. You have triggered their biggest fear of losing supply. They feel bad when they can't control you. Their egos get shattered, their self-esteem takes a dip, and they become angry, frustrated, and agitated. They feel clueless.

Narcissists will start blaming and gaslighting you for everything. They may often express that they do not feel loved. They will make you feel guilty and may become more passive-aggressive to disrupt your life and routine. They will use all sorts of tactics to bring you back under control. Silent treatment is often used as punishment, intending to induce guilt in you.

Narcissists will engage in smear campaigns to turn people against you. They will start looking for other sources of supply.

The most dangerous time in a narcissistic relationship is when you decide to leave the abuser. When you plan your exit and the narcissist somehow finds out, it becomes extremely dangerous. What makes it so perilous is their unpredictable and unstable nature. It doesn't matter what type of narcissist you're dealing with; all of them are capable of extreme cruelty. Narcissists generally prefer to maintain control in relationships and may even try to end the relationship themselves rather than being abandoned. They don't want to be left without supply. This is why, when they discover your exit plan, they lose control and may do terrible things.

Every move the narcissist makes is a performance, a bluff, a desperate little magic trick hoping nobody notices the wires holding it all together. They don't connect with people; they target them. It's not love, not care, not even curiosity—it's strategy, it's control, a sick little game masked as intimacy. While you feel deeply from your soul and carry real light in your chest, the narcissist is busy pulling strings, flipping switches, and testing people like lab rats. When they push people away, it isn't because they want solitude—it's because they need to see if you'll crawl back. It's manipulation dressed up as independence.

The narcissist questions every decision, lie, and fake smile but never reveals their doubt. Pride traps them, and fear is their leash. They walk around like they own the room, but deep down, they're one inch away from collapse. That fake confidence? It's a mask glued on with panic and ego. This is why you need to leave a narcissist—because they break you down before discarding you.

Narcissists will show their true colors at the end of the relationship. During this time, they reveal their darkest side. You will be treated as if you never did anything for them. They will blame and gaslight you for all the problems in the relationship. They will call you horrible and ungrateful, even comparing you unfavorably to their exes.

Narcissists won't be able to tolerate your presence. They may display aggressive and vindictive behavior, run smear campaigns, and arrange a support system to back them after discarding you—or forcing you to discard them. Sometimes, they simply disappear without explanation.

They will destroy your confidence and erode your self-esteem before leaving you.

Narcissists help others only to gain attention, admiration, validation, compliments, and appreciation—and to create an image of kindness. They help to gain control, and it makes them feel powerful. They want to show the world they are kind and loving, but they do nothing without motives. When they help, they make sure everyone knows. And they expect unconditional support and obedience from those they've helped.

Narcissists are selfish and cunning. When they help you, they want your loyalty and obedience. If you go against them, they will remind everyone of what they did for you and call you ungrateful.

If they spend money on you or help you in some way, they expect to take everything back in return—with interest. They invest little in you but expect maximum benefits. Narcissists always help people with selfish motives and hidden intentions.

Narcissists are exceptionally skilled at making others like them. Many are high-functioning individuals who appear normal, cordial, and admirable to others. This creates a profound disconnect for you as the victim, especially when you try to explain your suffering to others. Outsiders—whether friends, family, or acquaintances—may praise the narcissist as a wonderful person, which can lead others to question your sanity or accuse you of being ungrateful.

This dynamic is not exclusive to male narcissists. Many narcissistic women are equally adored by people outside the family, seen as accommodating, charming, and hospitable.

They often play the role of the perfect host, making it nearly impossible for others to believe the abuse happening behind closed doors.

When a narcissist decides "YOU'RE DEAD TO ME," it's their way of eliminating you from their existence once and for all. It typically comes after several silent treatments, pre-emptive discards, and plenty of verbal abuse and sabotage. This final discard is their ultimate gesture to erase the relationship from the face of the earth, as if it never existed. It releases them from any responsibility and ensures there is no chance of further contact.

Why does this happen with certain victims and not with others? It generally happens when the narcissist sees you as unavailable—maybe you're married, in a relationship, or you've rejected their advances. It can also happen if you've exposed them for who they truly are and challenged them over their behavior. As soon as they know you're on to them, you become a threat, and they feel the need to eliminate you from their life. Another scenario is that they've found someone else to manipulate—a "new supply" that they like better than you. To keep their new game going, they must push you out of the way.

Being "DEAD" to a narcissist is one of the most painful experiences. The one you loved becomes cold, detached, and uncompassionate. They may become angry and cruel toward you, making you feel worthless while acting like the victor. They often take pleasure in your pain, doubling their efforts to hurt you until you finally leave in peace. They don't care about your feelings, your perspective, or your truth. Their goal is to completely remove you from their life.

If this happens to you, I am truly sorry. It's a very painful process, and you will need healing time. Narcissists will not give you closure, answers, or apologies because they lack empathy. The person you thought you knew is gone. They will block or ignore you if you try to get in touch. If you challenge them, they'll dismiss you as though you don't exist. They may even bad-mouth you so that others think you're guilty or "insane."

It's hard to let go, but it's necessary. Take care of yourself by going no contact, seeking therapy, and taking care of yourself and loving yourself. Coming through this kind of betrayal is hard, but you are stronger than you think. You will survive; one step at a time.

We all have the power to build our self-confidence. Taking control of your self-confidence will help you take control of your life. Confidence and assertiveness are learned skills, and you can acquire and improve them through mindful and reflective practices.

How Do You Sound Confident?

- Overcoming fear
- Positive rephrasing and affirmations
- Setting goals
- Morning routines

Now, I want you to answer the above with: *Who, What, How, Where, and What for?*

Your thoughts have a powerful effect on shaping your confidence. Positive words and affirmations can significantly improve your confidence by breaking down negative beliefs that hold you back. Transforming your thoughts into positive ones enables you to concentrate on what is achievable rather than what seems limited. Negative beliefs create barriers, while positive thoughts keep you motivated toward your goals. By showing compassion to yourself, you can create an optimistic outlook.

Why should you set goals?

Achieving your goals boosts self-esteem. Goals must be measurable and align with your values. Knowing your path motivates you to reach milestones.

Visualization – When you visualize, you use your imagination to picture your success. You have the capacity to influence your objectives and shape your perception of challenging tasks. Observing your own success increases the likelihood of achieving these goals. This approach can also be applied to managing stress effectively.

How Do You Visualize? Steps To Help You Visualize:

- Decide what your goal is going to be.

- Envision the scene and what the environment might look like.

- Consider the steps that would make this moment successful.

- Continue to visualize these moments of success until it's time to make them happen.

- Approach the visualized situation with confidence.

Confronting your fears can lead to transformative outcomes. Fear undermines confidence, self-esteem, and success. One effective way to address these fears is to confront and acknowledge them. Understanding how fear is perceived can help you develop the confidence to try new activities and face challenges.

Questions To Ask Yourself:

- What exactly is your fear?
- Where did it come from?
- What would happen if you did not avoid this fear?
- What are the pros and cons of taking this risk?
- How can you overcome these fears?

Now is the time to reclaim your own life! Realize that a narcissist relies on you more than you rely on them, and their goal is to diminish your self-worth. You can now redirect your attention. It is time to reclaim your POWER. Focus on your inner strength to begin making changes. Celebrate your resilience and the courage it took to prioritize your well-being and mental health.

- Practice self-compassion. This is crucial in the healing process. Treat yourself with the same kindness and understanding you would offer to a friend in a similar situation.
- Establish boundaries to support your well-being.
- Define the behaviors and interactions you are willing to accept and communicate them clearly.

- Remember that boundaries are powerful for protecting your self-esteem and preventing future manipulation.

- Create a supportive network of family and friends. They remind you of your worth, making you feel valued and loved, which helps rebuild your self-esteem and promote a positive self-image.

- Be available to rediscover who you are. Engage in activities of interest or explore new ones.

- Explore those interests and passions so you can reconnect with your authentic self and rebuild your sense of identity.

- Challenge any negative self-talk by questioning its validity and replacing it with positive affirmations. Negative self-talk can undermine your self-esteem and keep you trapped in a cycle. Change your mindset to develop a positive self-image.

- If needed, seek professional help with your feelings and experiences. Professionals can give you coping skills to help you navigate the complexities of building your self-esteem.

- Focus on personal growth. Work on setting goals and committing to self-improvement. Identify areas of your life where you want to grow and take steps toward improvement.

- Focusing on personal growth allows you to take positive control of your future and create a healthier journey. It can boost your self-confidence and provide a sense of accomplishment.

- You are enhancing your abilities and strengthening your self-esteem. Don't procrastinate—you have a whole new life to look forward to!

Take your time before entering a new relationship. Healing from a narcissistic relationship requires patience and self-reflection. Rushing into a new relationship can hinder healing and repeat old patterns. Use this time to find out what you genuinely want from a partner and from relationships. Focus on building a solid foundation of self-love and self-awareness before seeking out a new romantic relationship. This approach will help you create healthier, more fulfilling relationships in the future.

Healing takes patience, self-compassion, and commitment to growth. By recognizing your pain, setting boundaries, and prioritizing self-care, you can reclaim your life and build a brighter future. You are worthy of love and happiness, and with time and effort, you can heal and move forward.

Seize the Time!!!

How Happy Are You?

---

1. I feel that life is very rewarding.

   - Always

   - Often

   - Sometimes

   - Rarely

   - Never

2. I can find the goodness in myself and others.

   - Always

   - Often

   - Sometimes

   - Rarely

   - Never

3. I am optimistic about the future.

- Always

- Often

- Sometimes

- Rarely

- Never

4. I take pleasure in everyday activities.

- Always

- Often

- Sometimes

- Rarely

- Never

5. I feel joy from moment to moment.

- Always

- Often

- Sometimes

- Rarely

- Never

6. I have a sense of meaning and purpose in my life.

   - Always

   - Often

   - Sometimes

   - Rarely

   - Never

7. I possess a significant amount of energy.

   - Always

   - Often

   - Sometimes

   - Rarely

   - Never

8. I can find the good, even in a demanding situation.

- Always

- Often

- Sometimes

- Rarely

- Never

9. I welcome and accept my feelings throughout any given

day.

- Always

- Often

- Sometimes

- Rarely

- Never

10. I actively keep in touch with friends and family.

- Always

- Often

- Sometimes

- Rarely

- Never

11. When things are tough, I reach out for support.

- Always

- Often

- Sometimes

- Rarely

- Never

12. I feel grateful for what I have.

- Always

- Often

- Sometimes

- Rarely

- Never

13. I let go of past disappointments or hurts.

- Always

- Often

- Sometimes

- Rarely

- Nevcr

14. I adapt to change very easily.

- Always

- Often

- Sometimes

- Rarely

- Never

Forgiveness Ritual (Say This To Yourself)

I Love You

I Am Sorry

I Forgive You

Thank You For...

Your Personal Mission Statement

Below, write down as many verbs that speak to you. Use verbs that are exciting or important to you.

Step 1

Choose three of your top verbs and write them here:

__________, __________, and _____________.

Step 2

What is a value you hold true?

What is a cause you believe in wholeheartedly, no matter what?

Is there a virtue that you hold true?

Write down your one core value.

Step 3

Who are you here to help? This can be a single person, a group of people, or an organization.

Write your cause word or phrase here: _________________

Step 4

These are the pieces to a story you are writing. Complete the sentences below and begin to live your life with purpose.

My mission is to (verb step 1) ______________, (verb step 1) ______________, and (verb step 1) ______________ with (step 2 core value/phrase) ______________ to (step 3 who you are here to help) ______________.

Gaslighting

Gas lighters are expert manipulators. They need control and power. They need to be in charge, and they need to be right about everything. They constantly criticize, blame, make abusive statements, intimidate, deny responsibility, and impose their judgment on you. Their behaviors often start off subtly and continue until they become abusive. They may find ways to credit themselves for your accomplishments, accuse you of having the issues they actually have, and often give you backhanded compliments.

Gaslighting isn't an isolated incident. It is persistent, insidious behavior that keeps you on edge, questioning yourself and those around you, while eroding your self-esteem and possibly your identity. Gas lighters often behave this way because they were raised by parents who gaslighted them, or because they seek control, power, or domination over their victims.

Certain mental health conditions, such as narcissistic personality disorder and antisocial personality disorder, lend themselves to gaslighting. These conditions give people a distorted view of themselves and others, along with a tendency to manipulate others for their own ends. They rarely acknowledge their own culpability or faults and instead project them onto others.

Typically, a gas lighter has a significant other who supports them under most circumstances. They will also use other people against you with comments like, *I'm not the only one who thinks you're wrong.* These may be lies or exaggerations, but they serve the gas lighter's purpose. They keep you isolated from family and friends, which gives them more control.

Gaslighting causes stress and emotional distress. Continuous exposure to verbal and sometimes physical abuse can erode your sense of identity, self-worth, and confidence. This may lead to additional mental health issues such as depression and anxiety.

Questions

Gaslighting is a form of psychological manipulation.

Gaslighting causes?

Gas lighters have certain mental health issues such as?

Gas lighters see themselves as?

What does gaslighting do to the victim?

Give an example of a gaslighting statement.

What Is Narcissistic Abuse?

This pattern of behavior is characterized by an exaggerated sense of self-importance, an ardent desire for excessive attention and admiration, and a significant lack of empathy toward others. Behind this mask is a person with fragile self-esteem that is vulnerable to the slightest criticism.

People With Narcissistic Personality Disorder (NPD):

1. Have an exaggerated sense of importance.
2. Want people to recognize they are superior.
3. Exaggerate their achievements and talents.
4. Envision scenarios of success, power, brilliance, beauty, or finding an ideal partner.
5. Believe they are superior and can only be understood by, or associate with, equally special people.
6. Require constant admiration.
7. Have a sense of entitlement.
8. Take advantage of others to get what they want.
9. Hide mistakes.
10. Lie to themselves and others.

11. Have an inability or unwillingness to recognize the needs and feelings of others.
12. Are envious of others and believe others envy them.
13. Behave in an arrogant manner.

Regardless of who you are dealing with, recognizing the patterns of narcissistic behavior is critical. Now you are on your way toward understanding, healing, and freedom!

People who have NPD are not aware that they have it. They believe they are not the problem—everyone else is. The disorder includes a lack of self-awareness, which makes it hard to manage.

Narcissists are expert manipulators who have honed their skills over the years and are incredibly charming, especially at the beginning of the relationship or when they want something. It is easy to get swept off your feet by this personality. That is how you got here! Over time, the mask begins to slip. It happens slowly, and one day you wake up and wonder how your life turned around. You feel emotionally charged all the time. Narcissistic people often choose partners who are highly successful and deeply empathetic.

Remember: Knowledge Is Power!

Understanding NPD better equips you to protect yourself, heal, and move forward with your life. You may have been walking on eggshells, constantly second-guessing yourself, or feeling like this emotional roller coaster never stops. Remember that abuse is not always physical. It may not be recognized as abuse, but it still causes distress to your self-esteem and sanity without leaving visible scars. This form of abuse is often subtle, elusive, and hard to recognize, especially when you are in the middle of it. It affects your psychological and emotional well-being and can be just as devastating as, or even more than, physical abuse. It gradually erodes your sense of self, your confidence, and your perception of reality.

Invisible Warfare

Jekyll and Hyde Act: Narcissists are often skilled with manipulation tactics known as *love bombing*. They shower you with attention, affection, and promises of a fabulous future. Once they have you hooked, the façade crumbles. The person you fell in love with is now a stranger.

Gaslighting: This is psychological manipulation where the narcissist attempts to sow seeds of doubt in your mind, making you question your own memory, beliefs and sanity. They may deny saying things you clearly remember, accuse you of overreacting, or flat-out tell you that your belief is wrong.

Blame Game: In a narcissist's world, they are never at fault. You are constantly braced for the next accusation. Gaslighting is a powerful tool that can make you question everything you know to be true—but that doesn't make your beliefs any less valid.

Rollercoaster: One minute they are singing your praises, and the next they are tearing you down. By keeping you constantly in a state of flux, they ensure that your attention stays fixed on them, which makes you off-balanced. This creates a cycle of dependency, leaving you off-balance and seeking their approval. It is a powerful control tactic that keeps you emotionally unstable—always hoping for the next high while bracing for the inevitable low.

Smear Tactic: Narcissists are often charming in public, but when they get home, they can be nasty. They may turn your friends and family against you. This isolation tactic makes you more dependent on them.

Silent Treatment: They may give you the cold shoulder for days, leaving you anxious and desperate for their attention.

Triangle Association: It may feel like there is a third person in the room. They may flirt with others or compare you to exes.

Financial Manipulation: They may withhold money, control finances, or run up debt in your name.

These patterns often creep up slowly, so you do not realize how bad things have gotten until you are in too deep.

When someone shows you who they are, believe them the first time. People know themselves much better than you know them. That is why it is important to stop expecting them to change. They are who they are!

What's The Cycle?

Honeymoon: This is where the "happily ever after" happens. The narcissist is on their best behavior, presenting the idealized version of themselves to hook you in.

Devaluation: Once they have you firmly in their grasp, their true colors begin to show. The person who once thought you were their dream now picks apart everything you do.

Discard: The narcissist may give you the silent treatment, openly flirt with others, or even leave you in public situations. They make you feel worthless and replaceable.

Hoovering

Just when you thought it was over and you started to pick up the pieces, they want back in your life. They apologize, promise to change, or remind you about the good times. Suddenly, they become the person you fell in love with again. They know exactly which buttons to push when they feel you slipping away.

The more you struggle, the deeper you sink. This creates a trauma bond—a powerful emotional attachment that forms in abusive relationships. It makes you addicted to the relationship. Remember, they are manipulating you; they are not in love. The only person who can break the cycle is you. You can stop the merry-go-round.

Yes, you invested so much time, energy, and love into this relationship. Walking away may feel like you gave up, but it's okay. It's actually a brave and necessary step toward reclaiming your life. Investing in yourself is not admitting defeat but choosing victory on your own terms. Leaving means stepping into the unknown, and that can feel scary. After years of belittlement and manipulation, your self-esteem may be at its lowest. Always remember: abuse is never the victim's fault.

If you have children, the stakes may feel even higher. You might worry about the impact of divorce on them or fear losing custody because of manipulation. But staying in an abusive relationship isn't healthy for your children. They see the pain and abuse. Narcissists often create financial dependence, making it even harder to leave. Think about the future—would you want your son or daughter to allow their significant other to treat them the same way?

Leaving a narcissist is like detoxing from a drug. It's hard, and you might relapse a few times before you are free for good. But on the other side of the pain is freedom, self-respect, and the chance to build a new life filled with genuine love and respect.

The Emotional Experience

Whatever you are feeling right now; it's okay. There is no "right" way to feel. Your emotions may be all over the place, and that's normal.

Grief: You're not just losing a partner—you're losing the dream of what your relationship could have been. You may be grieving the person you thought you were with—that charming person from the early days who turned out to be someone you no longer recognize.

Anger: You are angry with your ex for their manipulation and abuse, and angry with yourself for not seeing it sooner. That anger is perfectly justified. It's also a sign that you are starting to recognize your worth. Just don't let it consume you.

Fear: You may be afraid of being alone or of starting over. You may have financial fears, fears about your children, and fears about your future.

Relief: You may feel relief that the constant walking on eggshells is over. Relief that you don't have to pretend anymore. Your feelings are valid. The burden was heavy, and now you are putting it down.

Confusion: You may have contradictory thoughts and feelings. One minute you're sure you are doing the right thing, and the next you're second-guessing everything. With time and distance, this confusion will clear. This is a normal reaction to gaslighting and emotional abuse.

Guilt: You may feel guilty for "breaking up the family" or for "giving up." Remember, you did not cause this situation. You simply refuse to enable it any longer.

Loneliness: The absence of even an unhealthy relationship can leave you feeling empty. It's okay to feel that loneliness.

Hope: You may feel hope for a peaceful future, for genuine love, and for the chance to rediscover yourself.

Pride: You may feel pride in your strength, in your courage to leave, and in your resilience. Celebrate!

Numbness: You may feel like you are on an emotional roller coaster. That's okay. It can leave you feeling drained, confused, and unbalanced. You will have good days and bad days.

Trust your heart and be brave. Just when you think you are out, they may pull you back in with their mind games—manipulation and gaslighting. Gaslighting is a serious form of emotional manipulation that makes you question yourself, as if they are messing with your head.

Examples of Gaslighting:

- Your ex has a completely different recollection of your relationship.
- They portray themselves as the wronged party, trying to make you feel guilty for standing up for yourself.
- They bring other people into the conflict to support their version of reality.
- Just when you think you have reached an agreement, they change the terms.
- They deliberately provoke you and then accuse you of being "crazy."

While you are dealing with a divorce:

- Document everything.
- Limit your conversations.

- Build your support team.
- Trust yourself. Take a deep breath, remind yourself you are not crazy, and keep moving forward.
- Focus on self-care.
- Educate yourself on the legalities. Make sure your lawyer understands narcissistic personality disorder and your ex's tactics.

Remember, gaslighting and manipulation are designed to keep you off-balance, to make you doubt yourself so that you are easier to control. But you are the one in control now. You see the game they are playing, and you have the power. You are dealing with someone who is an expert at twisting things around. Stay strong and focused! You have already taken the hardest step by deciding to leave. Stay the course! Dust yourself off and start again.

Feelings Of Failure

Narcissists are experts at making everything your fault. They spend years drilling into your head that you are not good enough, that you are the problem, that if only you tried harder, loved them more, or were "better" in some way, things would improve. Look yourself in the mirror and say to yourself: *"I am God's child. I have faith."*

Many of us were taught that marriage is supposed to last forever. So when a relationship ends, especially a marriage, it can feel like a personal failure. But some relationships simply don't work out. That doesn't make you a failure; it makes you someone brave enough to admit that the relationship is not working.

Are you beating yourself up for not seeing the signs earlier? For staying too long? For letting yourself be manipulated? That's not fair to yourself. Had you known then what you know now, circumstances would have been different.

It's important to remind yourself that surviving a challenging situation is a testament to your resilience. Tell yourself: *"I am a strong, loving person with good health and a strong mind. I deserve happiness."*

Learn about narcissistic abuse and its impact on victims. Understanding this will aid your growth and transform you into a stronger, wiser person. Remember to love yourself and be patient during your healing journey.

Recognize who you really are and celebrate your strength. It takes great courage and strength to leave a narcissistic person and choose yourself. Every day you are confronted with fear—fear of the unknown, fear of failure, fear of being alone.. You are moving with the changes. You should be proud of yourself.

Healing is a process. It's like climbing out of a negative situation. You are doing the work! You are reading, seeking understanding, and searching for healing. You are looking in the mirror and realizing, *I love myself.* That is not only strength—it is wisdom!

You are rewriting your narrative, your story. You are surviving. It's like the twelve-step program—every day you keep moving is a victory. Celebrate small wins, practice positive self-talk, journal, and surround yourself with good people. Strength is about being broken and then putting yourself back together as a better version of who you are.

When you move on, individuals with narcissistic traits may respond in a variety of ways:

1. **Moving on greatly upsets a narcissist.**

   They get angry. Narcissists are very jealous and insecure. They can't handle seeing you living your life without them. They believe that once they've been part of your life, you belong to them forever.

2. **When you move on, the narcissist tries to pull you back.**

   They want to remain important in your life. They feel like you belong to them, so they don't want to let you go. They might already be saying terrible things about you to others to make you look bad. This way, when you try to move on, it seems like you're the one causing the problem, not them.

3. **When you move on, the narcissist keeps showing up in your life.**

They don't want you to forget about them. They are jealous and insecure and don't want you to be happy without them. They don't care about what you want; it's all about what they want.

4. They will stalk and bother you.

They won't leave you alone. They keep bothering you until you feel like the only way to make them stop is to talk to them or go back to them. They can't handle being left because they are afraid of abandonment. They believe that once they are in your life, they should be there forever—even if you don't want them to be.

Self-Care

Self-care is extremely important during this time. Ending a relationship with a narcissist is intense and draining. This is non-negotiable! Your stress levels are out of control, and self-care helps you manage stress before the stress manages you.

Regular self-care is essential for building emotional resilience to face life's challenges. Clear thinking is necessary for making sound daily decisions. It is also important to set and maintain boundaries. If you have children, it is crucial to demonstrate self-care and healthy coping strategies for difficult situations and decisions.

Although a busy schedule is common, achieving your goals is unattainable without self-care. Self-care encompasses daily activities. Personal transformation is contingent upon changing daily habits. The key to success lies in your routines and practices.

Experiencing anxiety and depression can be challenging. During these difficult times, it is important to use techniques to manage your emotions effectively. Practicing deep breathing can positively impact your body and help soothe your nervous system. Engaging in regular exercise and meditation can also provide significant benefits. Furthermore, maintaining mindfulness and being present in the moment are crucial practices.

It is important to carefully consider your interactions and commitments to maintain balance approach to coping. It is okay to say "No." Certain activities can be exhausting. Remember self-care.

When you say "No" to others, you are saying "Yes" to yourself. Love yourself—you are not selfish. Get at least eight hours of sleep to rejuvenate your body, brain, and soul. It takes time to manage anxiety and depression, so give yourself that time. Build your toolbox of coping strategies and use them consistently.

The goal is to keep moving forward in a positive way. Talk to a non-biased person, such as a therapist. You are building lifelong skills to become more resilient, to strengthen your self-esteem, and to have better emotional control. You are giving yourself the gift of personal growth.

Self-care is anything but selfish—it is one of the most important building blocks of fostering self-love, improving your relationships, boosting your creativity and productivity, enhancing your physical health, and so much more.

Reflection Questions:

- What is self-care and why is it important?
- What three self-care activities do you practice now?
- What new activities have you added to your consistent routine of self-care?
- How can you restructure your thinking process?
- Do you get annoyed or agitated easily?
- How stable are the foundations of your life?
- How secure do you feel about your home life, work life, and finances?
- How easily do you deal with sudden change?
- Do you avoid change, even when it could be positive, because you fear it?
- Do you persevere when striving for your goals?
- Do you feel supported in manifesting your goals? By whom?

What Is Post-Traumatic Stress Disorder (Ptsd)?

Are you missing your ex despite all that has happened? Surviving a relationship with a narcissist can leave lasting scars, such as:

- Flashbacks or nightmares about your relationship
- Feeling on edge all the time
- Avoiding people, places, or things that remind you of your relationship
- Negative thoughts
- Difficulty remembering

PTSD is your brain's way of trying to protect you from further harm.

What Is Trauma Bonding?

Experiencing feelings of missing an ex-partner, despite knowing their detrimental impact, is a common occurrence. This is often the result of trauma bonding, which arises from the repetitive cycle of abuse—including "love bombing" or intermittent periods of kindness. This cycle creates emotional highs and lows, which can become addictive.

To manage such feelings, ground yourself in the present moment, reframe memories with the reality of the relationship, and maintain no contact with your former partner. Surround yourself with supportive individuals, seek professional assistance, and educate yourself about PTSD and trauma bonding. These are essential steps. It is important to practice self-compassion and create new, independent memories. Progress in your healing journey is ongoing, leading to increased resilience, self-help strategies, and emotional intelligence that will benefit you throughout your life.

Make your written list. This may be difficult, but these are important items you will no longer have. Can you embrace unexpected changes and let things unfold naturally?

Stay calm and appreciate life even when things go wrong. Remember who you were before your narcissistic experience; joyful, humorous, and loving life. That person is still within you. Rebuild and embrace your true self.

Narcissists are like mirrors in the funhouse. They give distortions that have nothing to do with reality. It all comes from their insecurities.

What are five things you like about yourself?

What are things you are grateful for about yourself?

How are you going to celebrate those accomplishments?

Look in the mirror daily and tell yourself that you respect the decisions you are making and that you are worthy of love. These daily affirmations remind you of your worth.

Self-worth is not determined by others. You deserve love, kindness, respect, joy, and happiness. Ignore the negative voice that resembles your ex. Treat yourself well daily and give yourself compliments. Set boundaries, use positive language, say "No" when needed, and forgive yourself and your ex for past mistakes.

What Are Your Legal Rights?

Brace yourself! This is where things can get ugly! Have patience and self-control. Remember, you are fighting for you—for your authentic self. You may feel frustrated, and it may seem like an endless uphill battle. But you can survive, and you will survive.

Understanding the inner critic is important. The critical voice may not always reflect reality; it is simply a thought, and all thoughts can be altered. Observe the language you use when your inner critic starts pointing out perceived flaws. For every negative point it raises, look at your gratitude list and remind yourself of the good in your life.

Engage in the practice of observing your thoughts without judgment. This can assist in creating a separation between your identity and negative self-talk. When you find yourself being overly critical, consider asking, *"Will this matter tomorrow, in a year, or in five years?"* Look at the big picture!

Changing self-talk is a process. You must practice. With practice, you become more proficient. This is a special gift! Engaging in positive self-talk can enhance your performance across various aspects of your life. It is important to cultivate constructive self-dialogue as you strive for success. When faced with self-criticism, remember that you possess strategies to counteract negativity, and with consistent practice, you will manage these challenging thoughts effectively.

Boundaries protect you from negative energy and keep your newly rebuilt self-esteem safe and sound. Setting boundaries might feel uncomfortable at first, especially if you're not used to it. Different relationships require different boundaries. Customize your boundary for each relationship in your life. Boundaries are not about controlling others; they are about taking responsibility for yourself.

Boundaries are good for your relationships. Clear boundaries create clear expectations. Practice patience with yourself, as you have control over your environment and can decide who and what to allow in it. Your future self wants you to be confident and thriving. That version of yourself is exciting.

After surviving a relationship with a narcissist and navigating the divorce, you might feel like a stranger to yourself—as if you have been living someone else's life. Guess what? This is a new chapter in your life. All those dreams and passions are still there in the back of your mind. It's not about becoming a new person—it's about removing layers of control and manipulation to uncover the resilient self that has always been present.

Reconnecting with your interests is important. During your relationship with a narcissist, you might have felt like your identity was gone. But those passions are who you are. It's time to return to the things that were lost. This is your time to find yourself again, to explore and rediscover who you are. You may even discover new passions you never knew you had!

This journey is about rediscovering your authentic self. This is your journey. Embrace the process, celebrate the small stuff, recognize your victories, and have fun! You are not only reconnecting with your passions; you are also reconnecting with yourself.

Develop a strong support system. Research shows that people with strong support systems are more likely to have better mental health outcomes. Suppose you don't have a support system because your ex isolated you; know that you are brave enough to go out there and reconnect with the world. Take small steps. Join groups you might be interested in. Reconnect with old friends, they will be excited to see you. Connect with family members. Start a hobby. Shared interests are a great foundation for building friendships.

You may feel scared, but you will also feel more like yourself. You are rediscovering and remembering that you are a loving, interesting, and enthusiastic person. Remember to check the barometer when you are interacting with people.

- How do you feel? Do you feel drained or energized?

Healthy relationships take time.

- Are your interactions balanced?

- Are you always giving or taking?

- Is it a respectful relationship?

- Do you feel safe with them?

- Are you growing?

Be honest with yourself about your relationships. Be honest with yourself in your relationship. Don't be afraid to show your true self. Building a strong support system is key in your current development. You are moving on! It's okay to outgrow relationships or recognize that some connections aren't beneficial anymore. Your support system should be ever-evolving. It's normal to outgrow relationships, and your support system should adapt over time.

Are you prepared to start dating? Feeling apprehensive is natural when facing the unknown. Your previous relationship involved manipulation and emotional challenges. Apply your current knowledge and utilize the tools that help you become more secure. It's normal to feel fear, but don't let it control your future—use it to grow stronger.

Before you think about trusting someone else, it is crucial to rebuild trust in yourself. You are probably questioning your judgment.

Think back to your relationship with the narcissist.

Are you able to determine when a statement or situation lacks coherence?

Were you able to think through situations with a smile or a frown?

Did you suppress those feelings?

Did you second-guess your intuition?

Please provide some examples of those instances.

How does it make you feel?

Do you feel differently than you did when you were in that situation?

How would you react now?

Recognize your inner voice. Now you can listen to that voice more clearly and take a closer look.

In your journey to rediscover who you are, think of the areas of boundaries. One of the things you have learned is what your boundaries are. Protect them: your energy, your values, and your sense of self. What are your non-negotiables? In a potential partnership, they are how you want to be treated and what you are willing to accept in your relationship.

Answer the following questions. These are your worth:

• What behaviors are you no longer going to tolerate?

• How do you want to feel?

• What is your purpose in your life now?

• What are your non-negotiables?

In a narcissistic relationship, you might find yourself stressed and longing for a connection with your partner. Now you oversee you. Remember, you are in school again—you are not just dating, you are finding your authentic self. Don't rush. Practice setting boundaries and enjoy the process without stress or pressure.

It's okay to tell someone you want to pace yourself as you learn yourself. Build trust and respect in your new relationship. This is the foundation of a solid partnership. Be friends first before you get romantically involved. Continue building your friendships, hobbies, personal growth, and networks. Remember, you are adding to your life. Trust your intuition! You are opening yourself up to the possibility of a new and healthy relationship. That relationship will not flourish if you are not continuously building yourself.

Answer these questions. DREAM! They can come true.

- What do you dream about?

- What do you want?

- What does it feel like?

- Where are you going?

- How are you going to get there?

Now let's make those DREAMS into goals.

What do you want first? Identify your top three desires from your answers. These are your goals. Break them into smaller steps and decide how to progress towards them one step at a time.

As you embark on building a new life and a new self, it is essential to set timelines with patience and understanding. Visualizing your goals is a powerful step. Make it a habit to review them daily. Through this process, you will discover new aspects of yourself, experience personal growth, form meaningful friendships, and encounter new experiences you may not have previously imagined.

As you grow and change, your dreams might change, which is fine. Keep moving forward, guided by your own dreams, goals, desires, and aspirations—not someone else's!

You now understand that the problem was never yours—it was the toxic relationship you were trapped in. Validate the emotions you have been navigating. Your feelings are a testament to your ability to love, hope, and heal. You are now armed with tools to protect your mental health. You've learned to shield your mind from manipulation and gaslighting.

Manipulation involves tactics that lead you to trust the manipulator while questioning your own perceptions. Gaslighting means manipulation. A verb is used to describe the act of influencing another individual to question their own emotions, experiences, or perception of events. This is mental and emotional abuse designed to plant seeds of self-doubt and alter your sense of reality.

You may remember or have forgotten the conversation differently, or you may have no recollection at all. In recovery, you identify that the narcissist is insecure and shameful—not you. Always remember to detach and stop believing or reacting to falsehoods. It's because of the narcissist's character. It is not you, nor can you change someone. For a narcissist to change, it takes willingness and effort from both parties. Sometimes, when one person changes, so will the other. Typically, the other person has a personality disorder, and it's hard for them to change.

Take control of your financial future. Creating a budget and making financial decisions are steps toward regaining independence. Utilize strategies for co-parenting with a narcissist to ensure a safe, loving, and peaceful environment for your children. Building self-esteem involves setting boundaries and developing a strong foundation. Rediscover and map out your authentic self through thoughtful actions. You are looking to the future, turning pain into growth, and learning how not just to survive but to thrive. You now hold the hidden treasures in this journey. You've learned how to weather the storm, dance in the rain, and turn challenges into opportunities. You have walked through fire and come out thriving. You are the architect of your story, your life—of new beginnings and brighter tomorrows.

Challenges and periods of uncertainty may arise, and there will be times when the demands feel considerable. However, you possess the necessary tools, knowledge, and self-awareness to address any obstacles ahead. On occasions when doubt emerges or circumstances become overwhelming, it is important to remember that you are supported by a dedicated team—you are not navigating this journey alone. While your former partner may have sought to document aspects of your experience, the responsibility for shaping your narrative now rests with you. You have the opportunity to determine how the next chapters unfold, guided by self-confidence and resilience. This journey forward reflects your commitment to growth and empowerment.

Things To Remember

- You are stronger than you know. The fact that you are here reading this book is a testament to your incredible strength. You have survived the unimaginable, and that resilience will carry you to the next level.

- Your worth is not decided by others. No matter what your narcissistic ex may have told you, your value is intrinsic. It doesn't depend on anyone's approval or validation. You are worthy of love, respect, and happiness simply because you are you.

- You deserve peace and joy. After the storm you've weathered, you might feel guilty for wanting happiness. You've earned every moment of peace and every burst of joy that comes your way.

- Your past does not define your future. What happened to you is part of your story, but not your entire story. Your future is unwritten and full of possibilities. You have the power to shape it.

- Healing is not linear. Some days you will make progress, and other days you may experience setbacks. It's okay. Healing is a journey, not a destination. Every step, no matter the direction, is still moving forward and still progress.

• It is important to remember that you are not alone. Even in difficult times, you have a community of individuals who understand and empathize with your situation. Reach out and connect, allowing their resilience to support and guide you.

• Your voice matters. You may have been silenced, but you hold power. Your voice represents many people. Use it. Share your story, as I am. Your words can be a lifeline to others who need your help.

• It's okay to put yourself first. Self-care isn't selfish. Prioritizing yourself is okay, it is necessary for your growth and healing journey.

• Your vulnerability is your strength. Opening up about your experiences allows you to feel and heal. This takes courage. Your vulnerability is not a weakness; it is your power.

• You have everything you need within you to move to the next level: the resilience, the strength, and the wisdom to heal and thrive. You've got this.

• Small steps lead to big changes. Don't underestimate the power of these steps or actions. Each boundary you set, each re-affirming thought, each moment of self-care is one more step toward your celebration.

- The best is yet to come. Your best days are ahead of you. You are not surviving anymore; you are thriving!

I am so thrilled to see you healing. Healing is about unveiling the strong, fabulous soul that was always there beneath the layers of abuse and self-doubt. It's about reclaiming your life, your joy, your freedom, and your power.

Who I Am Now

Instructions: Utilize the following words to articulate your current self-description. Remember, no negative thoughts.

- What is your purpose?

- What's not working?

- Communicate your boundaries.

- Are you secure in your decision-making?

- The goal is to have inner peace.

Owning My Story

- Accountability
- Forgiveness for Self
- Trust for Self
- Healthy Relationships
- Partner
- Invest in Self
- Finding Peace for Yourself
- Letting Go

Journaling

Why is journaling so important? Journaling is an incredibly effective tool for self-discovery, personal growth, and emotional well-being. It provides a private and non-judgmental space where you can freely express your thoughts, process complex emotions, and reflect on your experiences. By documenting your daily challenges, successes, and moments of joy or discomfort, journaling encourages you to examine your thought patterns, emotions, fears, desires, behaviors, and goals in depth.

Writing things down helps you gain clarity about situations that may feel overwhelming, allowing you to identify triggers, patterns, and the consequences of your actions. It also enables you to explore how your behavior—and that of others—contributes to your reactions and outcomes. This practice fosters mindfulness, encouraging you to stay present and intentional in your actions, while paving the way for greater self-awareness and understanding.

Additionally, journaling serves as a record of your journey, giving you the opportunity to track progress over time and celebrate your growth. It can also help you set goals, define priorities, and develop a deeper connection with yourself. Overall, it is a transformative tool that promotes mental clarity, emotional resilience, and a sense of inner peace.

What Is Your Relationship With Yourself?

- Focus on the Victories.
- The Outcome of your Victory is Success!
- Let go of Negative Thinking. See the Success and Positive Outcomes.
- Do Not Settle! Expand your Thinking.
- Thrive on your Success.
- Sometimes say "No."
- Set Boundaries.
- Stay True to Yourself.
- Manifest Greatness.
- Visualize and Meditate on who you are and who you want to become.
- Maintain a clear focus. Be thankful for who you are and what you aspire to achieve.
- It is essential to believe in your goals. Express gratitude and visualize your objectives.
- Pay attention to the details.
- Don't start with negative thoughts. Use positive affirmations.

- Start with "I Am…"

Visualization

What is visualization? It is the practice of imagining what you want. It's the manifesting of your goals. It helps you establish what you want to achieve. It involves using your five senses—sight, feeling, hearing, touching, and smelling. This directs your subconscious mind to be aware of the end goal you have achieved or have in mind.

By building a greater understanding of your life, you can explore your inner self more clearly. Let go of the past. Forgive yourself and others.

What does forgiveness look like for you?

What is working for you?

If something is not working for you, fix or change it! (Be honest.) Visualize that which does not work for you going away.

Embrace self-reflection as a powerful tool for growth. Regularly assess your thoughts and actions, identifying patterns that serve your purpose and those that hold you back.

It is through this introspection that clarity emerges, guiding you toward meaningful change.

Harness the power of affirmations to strengthen your resolve. Speak boldly and confidently about what you want to become. Phrases like *"I am capable"* or *"I am worthy"* shape your emotions and thoughts, instilling a sense of empowerment that propels you forward.

Remember, the journey to achieving your aspirations requires persistence and adaptability. Accept challenges as opportunities for learning, and celebrate small victories along the way. Each step brings you closer to the life you envision, and each moment is a chance to reaffirm your dedication to your goals.

What is your purpose?

Don't hold yourself back. Step through the door. It may be difficult, but you will find confidence within. Be true to yourself.

What are you grateful for?

Be grateful for what you have—for yourself and for others.

Road To Self-Love

1. I appreciate how special I am.
2. Smother yourself in affirmation. (You are retraining your brain. Write affirmations, live them, feel them for them to work.)
3. Do things you love. Increase your joy daily. Make changes to do the things you love.
4. Find a replacement for negative thoughts.
5. Let the Love in and be Thankful to others and yourself. Make your body happy.
6. Don't compare yourself to others.
7. Forgive yourself and don't feel guilty.
8. Love yourself—soften your heart to receive love in order to give love.

Remember: thoughts → beliefs → habits → reality.

What Are Triggers?

Triggers are anything—a sound, a smell, a place, or even a situation—that brings up a strong emotional reaction tied to past experiences. For people who have experienced trauma, triggers can make it feel like the past is happening all over again, leading to anxiety, panic, or shutting down. Learning to recognize triggers is an important part of healing because it helps you build awareness, develop coping strategies, and regain a sense of control over your emotions.

When you are triggered, you lose your capacity for rational thought. Your prefrontal cortex (the thinking part of the brain) gets hijacked by your limbic system (the reacting part of the brain), blocking your ability to effectively problem-solve, listen, advocate for change, or carry on a productive conversation. Learn the triggers that change your behavior.

Internal Triggers

An internal trigger comes from within. It can be a memory, a physical sensation, or an emotion. For example, if you are exercising and your heart starts pounding, the sensation might remind you of a time you were running from an abusive partner. Other common internal triggers include:

- Anger
- Anxiety
- Feeling overwhelmed, vulnerable, abandoned, or out of control
- Loneliness
- Muscle tension
- Memories tied to a traumatic event
- Pain
- Sadness

In the context of mental health conditions, internal triggers are the cognitive and emotional cues that can lead to a relapse of symptoms. For example, negative thoughts and feelings might trigger a relapse of drug or alcohol use.

External Triggers

External triggers come from your environment. They can be a person, a place, or a specific situation. What may be a normal, everyday situation or a minor inconvenience for some may be triggering for someone living with mental illness or living with trauma.

For example, you may be triggered by:

- A movie, television show, or news article that reminds you of the experience

- A person connected to the experience

- Arguing with a friend, spouse, or partner

- A specific time of day

- Certain sounds that remind you of the experience

- Changes to relationships or the ending of a relationship

- Significant dates, such as holidays or anniversaries

- Going to a specific location that reminds you of the experience

- Smells associated with the experience, such as smoke

Think about your triggers, process them, and then write down your triggers below.

The Only Way Forward Is Developing Your Self-Esteem

You cannot alter anyone else's behavior, and your affection does not affect a narcissist. The validation they require is solely their own. Today, recognize that the path to progress lies in affirming your worth, value, and inherent love. It is essential to overcome the self-doubt you once carried.

Today, cease attempting to conform to a role that does not belong to you. It is imperative to embrace freedom and break away from constraints. This is your life, and you possess the right to self-love and self-appreciation. Is this a narcissistic response? No—it is simply an acknowledgment that you are sufficient. In order to extend love to others, you must first cultivate self-love.

Reflection Template

1. Title & Date

2. Situation / What was being discussed (1–2 lines — factual)

3. What I observed (facts, triggers, behavior's — no judgment)

4. What I felt (name emotions clearly)

5. What I thought (interpretations, beliefs that showed up)

6. What I learned / new insight (one or two sentences)

7. Evidence of growth (small wins, decisions, changes in reaction)

8. One concrete next step (one small action you will actually do)

9. Gratitude / affirmation (a sentence that reminds you of your values)

Your opinion matters! Please take a moment to leave an honest review we truly appreciate your support